THE DARK EDGE

OF THE BLUFF

THE DARK EDGE
OF THE BLUFF

poems

ELLENE GLENN MOORE

GREEN WRITERS PRESS

Brattleboro, Vermont

Printed in the United States

10 9 8 7 6 5 4 3 2 1

Green Writers Press is a Vermont-based publisher whose mission is to spread a message of hope and renewal through the words and images we publish. Throughout we will adhere to our commitment to preserving and protecting the natural resources of the earth. To that end, a percentage of our proceeds will be donated to environmental activist groups. Green Writers Press gratefully acknowledges support from individual donors, friends, and readers to help support the environment and our publishing initiative.

GReen
wrITers
press

Giving Voice to Writers Who Will Make the World a Better Place
Green Writers Press | Brattleboro, Vermont
www.greenwriterspress.com

ISBN: 978-0-9982604-5-7

COVER PHOTO BY THE AUTHOR

PRINTED ON PAPER WITH PULP THAT COMES FROM FSC-CERTIFIED FORESTS, MANAGED FORESTS THAT GUARANTEE RESPONSIBLE ENVIRONMENTAL, SOCIAL, AND ECONOMIC PRACTICES BY LIGHTNING SOURCE. ALL WOOD PRODUCT COMPONENTS USED IN BLACK & WHITE, STANDARD COLOR, OR SELECT COLOR PAPERBACK BOOKS, UTILIZING EITHER CREAM OR WHITE BOOKBLOCK PAPER, THAT ARE MANUFACTURED IN THE LAVERGNE, TENNESSEE PRODUCTION CENTER ARE SUSTAINABLE FORESTRY INITIATIVE® (SFI®) CERTIFIED SOURCING.

ACKNOWLEDGMENTS

Grateful acknowledgement is made to the editors of publications in which these poems first appeared, sometimes in earlier versions or under different titles:

Bluestem: "At Grand Hotel Poseidon, Paestum"
The Hopper: "At Carinae Viñedos, Mendoza"
Salamander: "At a Bike Shop in Faubourg Marigny," "In Shark Valley, Florida," "At Baker's Haulover Inlet"
Scalawag: "To Build a Fire"
The Stockholm Review of Literature: "After a Dinner at the American Embassy"

CONTENTS

THE DARK EDGE

OF THE BLUFF

POINT OF SAIL (I)

Leaving the mainland, this inlet rolls into the bay,
slight gasps of grass and bights
checkered onto the watery belly of the sky.
The clouds are as unaffected as planets,
impassive mobiles of water and light, as if
an unbearable weight were suspended in our minds.
For days I have been circling
around a question of balance—that red mobile
wavering in an empty wind—
or times I jumped from my childhood bed and knew
with no small certainty
I had been flying,
if only for one moment—
so many days on the floor of my bedroom,
spinning and spinning,
waiting for something to rise up in me,
the laws of my whirring universe.
I learned to ride a bike
carrying a galaxy in my belly.
In a book, I examined a diagram of a bicycle wheel,
searching for an answer
to the water churning inside me,
or why the spinnaker moon follows us,
window to window, from one end of the house to the other,
or how we now stay upright
as you cut the motor
and fling the mainsail open into wind.
Exposed this way, we are drawn

into the sun's ruddy invective like fish
slipping into unruly currents.
Running before the wind you say,
and I hug myself while the fiberglass hull hums
over the open face of the bay.
We can see the bottom,
sunken islands of seagrass bending in and out of focus,
like the ragged coasts of continents under a mapmaker's loupe.
I won't go in the water here,
but in the space between the bow and cresting waves
that is far too large for my body,
I lean back and wonder
how the wind carves rooms in our sails,
synaptic crossings of halyard, sheet, and mast.
Once as a child I looked up into the unimaginable geometry
of the National Gallery atrium, Calder's honeycomb mobile
revolving in invisible columns of air,
filling the space with lungs, wings, suns—like thoughts
converging and digressing in murmurs.
I return there when I crave an answer.
I, too, am revolving.

WHALE WATCHING IN EARLY SPRING

I.

We weren't expecting this drought, the coolness
of the morning lacing its fingers through afternoon,
the road crisp as an apple peel. We follow one clean
turn after another, stop in a field scooped from powerlines.
It's a rocky strand, plump with strange seals,
the sound of sky bearing down on us. The rocks, oxalis,
the ruddy path. We are gasping for distant waves, that wild
air, unsure of our place between sand and pine.

II.

I make you sit behind the wheel while I examine
a dusty berm brimming with rosy-headed succulents.
This close drop into cold water, tender mustard
blossoms, full pine, that sweet-smelling ache.

III.

Once, we think we see a whale breach,
as dark as a thought surfacing, rolling into expression.

IV.

I am no mountain,
I am no open sea.

AT A BIKE SHOP IN FAUBOURG MARIGNY

And then: an old man and I looked through the scrap pile in the back, sifting through lonesome reams of brake pads and spools of cable housing, orphan top tubes, wheels, tires deflated and folded over themselves like cordgrass bent beneath the bellytrail of some slow bayou beast making its way to the river. Hefting a half-built bike up to the steel stand clamp, the man said *There's only one rule: Don't let the levee* bust. Beneath his white face a longing, something thick ebbing between us. He kept a bum hand in his pocket, hobble-tripped to a bin damp with river and leaking viscous oil. The bike's naked wheel spun in air sliced with a fan's sharp and rollicking breath. Plumes of dust eddied in the river-soaked light, flooding our hands with nothing we could hold.

AT THE FRIENDS' BURYING GROUND

I remember mapping the night sky
in correctional-orange flags in a field
in the middle of town. Here the universe expanded
only as far as the weathered limbs
of the grey fence that cracked dolefully around us,
summer children barred from traffic,
those celestial question marks
running across our dim horizon,
or liquid motes always just outside our field of vision.
The sky compressed to a salty landscape
as we marked the distance between stars
with our small, efficient pacing.
In the corner of that field we discovered spotty headstones
all catty wonk like broken fingers.
Even in that space, questions of silence
interrogated our small games.
This was the summer an island girl showed me
the hole in the hedge
to a broad garden beyond,
ragged with rosehip and magnolia,
and she told me to run *wicked fast* and I imagined
the wind knocking us over and blowing us across the grass,
gathering and scattering us with oak leaves and wilted petals
like the smattering of pinprick lights
in the sky, the real sky, larger
than our measures and markings, our small claims
on the voids echoing inside of us.
Who knew what worlds folded into themselves

beneath the softly rolling hills
where we charted the bodies of our known universe:
here, Neptune, a flag springing to perpetual life,
utterly plastic among the salt-aged stone,
and here, the Milky Way, a fluid stretch of caution tape
that wound through the blades of grass
like a stray hair curling on a pillow.
And here, just the moon echoed from our bedroom windows,
paper plate held down by a stone,
just big enough, we were learning,
to pull the ocean to its feet.

MILLENNIUM

At dinner I turned from the adult travelers,
older, warmer, more sure than I.
A burlap dog lifted its head, sniffed
and whimpered when I poured candlewax into my palm,
the small light splitting itself through my fingers,
splaying the ghost of my hand against the wall.
The glasses gathered on the table, tall as cypress trees,
overflowing with effervescence.
How I wanted to hold something ecstatic and pulsing.
When the evening deepened I stood with the others,
barefoot on the flagstone in my small pajamas,
chilled like the crisp bottles of gold
the adults passed between themselves.
I tipped my shoulders over the balcony,
watching fireworks sprout all over the countryside,
a luminous harvest of light and ash
scythed from the sky in wide, sparking arcs
bartering in light, negotiating
in phosphorescent hope for this hour,
sky spread beneath it like a warm lover.
My insides fizzed like the swallow of champagne
I finally coaxed from my mother's fluted glass.
I held my hand out against the horizon,
hoping to catch a seed of light.

TWO VIEWS OF ENCINITAS

Preoccupied for some time by the hills,
I finally turned to see the Pacific—just there!—stretched
in languid low tide, ebbing and returning as light
from the horizon. Light
plays differently here, you said,
although admittedly I may only have heard
what I wanted to hear.
But nonetheless—the light, the light,
and the buildings all mustard and tangerine,
I thought, sun-stunned and turning
from east to west.
No, I remember now you didn't mention the light,
but even you couldn't deny how it changed us.
For two hundred yards, it seemed,
the sand was spare as bone
in the light's low gaze
as all day I wove towards that smell,
warm pitch spiced with Torrey pines,
needles threaded through the late and blossoming dark,
pulling like a loose thread,
cauterizing the coastal tides,
the salt, the pine spice—and all those homes!—
the blond wood,
light from the west like a blood orange,
oxalis flaming the berms.
I will tell you what I wanted to say,
standing beside the sheer cliffs below Encinitas
as early spring returned

in a kind of swell of light from the sea—
the ocean, its grand-stand audacity,
thrilled with light,
the water so cold,
the luminous, fine-threaded mist
of distant waves, or thoughts, or whales.
If I believed my thoughts for a moment
longer than necessary, it was only a matter of survival:
attending to a memory of the impression of light,
which is itself only a memory of that sun,
bending around the horizon.
We may have told these stories to the ocean,
or it to us, some slight testament to the ache in our mouths.
Strutting out from the rock,
wry staircases of western pine
switchbacked down the face of the bluff.
It was all about that kind of restlessness, I think,
how we turned and returned,
like a memory: two views,
threaded through each other,
of ourselves at sunset at Encinitas, both
as real and as tenuous as that light
pivoting between sea and hills.

IN SHARK VALLEY, FLORIDA

There: at mile twelve we stopped at the chattering of some small trees, distant against the low sky doubling itself across the shallow waters of the swamp. *What kind are they?* I asked. *Ibis? Egret?* Heavy in the brush, an alligator grunted. We phosphoresced in the noon sun, praying with small breaths, hot, feathery seeds sticking like tattoos to the sweat on our necks. In a heave, then, the trees split open, releasing a hundred white slips into the sky. The empty branches hunkered down as though for sleep, horizon printed with saw grass, bromeliad, the dark thumbs of cypress. We shivered in the sun, thickened our breath, pressed our pedals forward like a heart beating against bone.

AT CARINAE VIÑEDOS, MENDOZA

Too late in the season for glimpses of fat gatherings
of Malbec or Cabernet, varietals burgeoning
in the astringent dust of the Uco Valley,
this warm easing-out of fall
basks the mountains in a light almost palpable,
the last twists of red and yellow of the vineyards, arched
espaldero style, protecting the yield from a rare sun
we have not yet come to know.

But we have gone up into the mountains,
prayed at their feet and let our hands wander
over the desert plants: tawny heads of grasses,
vegetal trumpets, grey and yellow
as a taste of sun bristling
from behind the low stratus of afternoon.

Now there is nowhere we can go
outside the full-bellied embrace of those mountains,
their bristles and turnings, flooded with afternoon light.
All of the light here is that particular amber,
that maceration of skin and stem,
the world tilting away, loving its own shadow.

AFTER A DINNER AT
THE AMERICAN EMBASSY

Now the Hotel Talleyrand squares behind my mother and me,
the lights on its blonde face bright as the bubbles
in our abandoned drinks.
We leave the reception, the bus,
the voice of the man with the turned leg
who for six days has ushered us into and out of
and up and down. Everyone
has commented on my dress, my mother's stories,
our place settings littered with spoonfuls
of chilled soups, saccharine voices, the wrappers of petit fours.
Now we wrap ourselves,
my thin shawl a small comfort,
a tomato skin blanched and bathed in ice, slipped
from a shivering and tender orb, roadmap of membranes,
thin as the veins on my mother's exposed wrist
as she slips a cigarette from its pack.
The bus pulls away from the curb,
leaving us to step into the street towards the river.
A taxi skirts the corner
and my mother throws out her arm,
holds me back
from its blaring headlights.
I notice her hands,
think of how once when I was small
she slapped my face
when I pressed our old phone's hook switch, disconnecting
her long distance call.

My skin burned. I don't know
why I did it, but perhaps I craved her voice,
how at night she wove her childhood into smoke-darkened
    stories,
sitting on the side of my bed.
Now the streetlamps at the Place de la Concorde swallow us,
swallow the sky, the muted stars.
Their incandescent globes make their own
celestial bodies, cosmos
cupped in the city's mouth.
My mother breathes,
stamps the cigarette under her squat heel.
Now, silence on the tips of our tongues,
we turn from the water, its obsidian curves,
to the Eiffel Tower rising over the 7th arrondissement.
What if I say it illuminates
just as we step beneath its cavernous belly?
That a woman sings *Lakmé* from some tired window?
Now in the fading street
her tourmaline voice gathers us, the lights,
the lattice dome of puddled iron,
the chattering night that breaks over
my mother and me.
In my bag I have collected small papers, tickets,
an over-sized postcard of the tapestry at Bayeux,
a story of horses and ships and kings.
We must worship something.

AT GRAND HOTEL POSEIDON, PAESTUM

Here, the hotel owner's daughter kissed my brother on the cheek
after we raced the glass elevator up and down the stairs,
skidding in patterned ankle socks along the red carpet
until we were banned from taking the elevator at all.
Which didn't stop the girls from giggling *Ah,*
such ladies' man, such charming,
and I thought of how the daughter's cropped hair curled darkly,
soft at the nape of her neck.
On the beach we stretched out towels striped in blue and white,
stolen from our hotel shower stands and aching for sun.
Even our small bodies craved something bright
for the emptiness spilling out of our mouths.
Under the fan of grape leaves a busboy loosened his collar,
tossed his handful of crumbs into the flowerbed,
saying *Hey, Cutie, where you from?*
Down the curve of the beach a woman removed her bikini top.
We stared with our mouths, sat on our hands.
How golden she was, lit from within,
hard and precious like slow pitch, amber, basalt.
Planks nestled in the sand guided us towards the water,
and my brother, rubbing his cheek, slipped in.
I followed, pinched and pulling at the swimsuit stretched over
    my belly,
full of bread with pressed olives and red wine vinegar,
the same red that poured into my brother's face
where the owner's daughter lit her kiss,
before we tore down the sand-spiked street to the sea
so full of salt, they said,
we would bob high on our backs like corks.

WALKING TOUR

This is why we are here in the first place,
marching into our own distractions,
eating sweet media lunas with something hot,
sugar roasted with the whole bean,
this burnt maw of autumn inviting us closer.
To what, we aren't sure, but beneath
a wrought iron transom proclaiming *Mercado*
you worry the loose button on your coat
and I let my fingers find the tattered lining of your pocket,
hollow now for the 200 pesos you handed
the tour guide as explanation for our early departure
from political voyeurism and our own discomfort.
At a bistro I savor an ink-black taste of ocean
and a boy whose sweater unravels at the hem
asks you a question we can't comprehend in any language.
When he bare-hands the steak from your plate
I watch his shoulders shrink and we are confused
by our feelings of having been violated
because you were through with lunch, anyway.
We are unsure what to do
with this tepid sense of loss rising within us,
which we fear like slick leaves on the sidewalk,
and even the sun's familiar fire
paints the street a color we would never try to name.
Walking down the Avenida de Mayo
we can only demonstrate
the wide-handed tourism of our age and means,
looking up and looking down, resting finally

in the plaza scattered before the Casa Rosada
where Las Abuelas mourn, their soft kerchiefs
emblazoned onto the ground like a map
directing us to someone else's grief.

TO BUILD A FIRE

70 miles from Valdosta we negotiate the swollen dusk
of the Okefenokee, bald cypress and Virginia chain
rising from the water in dark striations,
stripping the sky of its waning light. Five of us

packed tight in the car: mother and father,
my two brothers and me, stuffed between hollow
talk, shoes and tents. The tape deck whispers
about a nameless man lighting matches in the snow,

wondering if he should kill his dog. Fighting sleep,
I bury my fingers in my lap, shrink against the car door
as night thickens. The nameless man aches for warmth.
We build our own fire, a mouth spitting ash towards the trees

while thumb-sized blue crabs scuttle, claws tight
and snipping at pinprick glints of dust and sand.
They sidle away from our light
to the impenetrable pitch of the swamp. I find

a branch of sweetbay splayed into brown, clacking blades,
drag it over the sand to make cities for ants,
let the firelight shine through my hands.
How remote we are, I think, though only six plots away

the camping office brightens the pine with lamps
lit like eyes in the windows. Our fire burns
until we are done. Poor, poor nameless man.
Didn't anyone teach you not to travel alone?

Didn't anyone teach you to stay warm?
Miles from highway, the stars are excruciating.
We crawl into our tents, collapse in borrowed heat.
We wring ourselves like worn gloves.

MEDITATION ON DISTANCE

Longing, we say, because desire is full of endless distances.
—ROBERT HASS, *"Meditation at Lagunitas"*

If longing is a kind of damage,
there is too much damage to chart—
widowmaker caught
in the arms of a white cedar,
widow's peak, which means something
the way the Wife of Bath's gap tooth
means desire (so much, it seems,
means desire: the pattern of leaves
on the hood of a blue Ford,
or the ring of scale left in the porcelain sink)—
and widow walks with their functionless charm.
No one to watch for, no boat
birthed from the horizon.
Distance cuts both ways, I'm afraid—
desire for fullness and desire to be bereft,
and desire itself is both
as whole as the ocean
and empty as the space curled beneath a wave.
Is it helpful to look for signs,
to perceive meaning in the number of fingers,
held against the horizon,
between that wind-savaged sail
and the lighthouse on the bluff?
Or to wonder how many pennies,
flung from the rail of the ferry
as it rounds Brant Point,
have kissed the object of their desire
before going down?

Gravity alone will not cause motion; this is true
of any object—loose branch seized with potential,
a leaf on the edge of breaking,
water swirling around its center.
And, of course, the stars.
Are they as strange as you imagined?
A scythe of light from the point splits open the sky
like Athena splitting Zeus's head in her fury for clarity.
I never know if that light is a warning or a promise.
Not everything is about longing.
Distance, alone, will not cause desire.
Along the coast,
a freshwater lake is separated from the ocean
by a spit of sand just wide enough to walk over.
Does the fresh water crave the big water's salt,
its tang, its body
moving under the sun?
All day across the surface of the lake,
the little sailboats scud back and forth,
failing to etch a permanent line.

BUENOS AIRES LOVE POEM

The cab makes one breakneck turn
after another and while I don't believe
we are going to die, pressed into each other,
here, in this chilled backseat June
two thousand miles south of the equator,
I do have my worries. And I can't help
but wonder at the Recoleta lights shouting
out of wrought iron windows as we careen
down Avenida Corrientes and then the low,
cold midrise lights of Avenida Sarmiento
where we are deposited, spun like wheels
over asphalt into the center of Almagro
and into a milonga, voices dimmed,
with a wood floor shuffled smooth,
chandelier in fabric, a tattered heart lit
like a bloodless sun above our heads,
pilgrims of candlewax and a sweet torrontés
we coax out of tea cups
in junkyard chairs. And when we are warm
we learn to walk not in a line, like the moon
carefully adhering to the sun,
but in the manner of constellations
that pitch and yaw with the tilt of the earth,
expansive as this city,
as indelible as its lights
after we close our eyes.

AT BAKER'S HAULOVER INLET

You tell me this: the inlet was not carved from this spit of land by glaciations, frozen inching of big water. Not the insistences, waves, the riving wind-limned eye of a storm. But rather, the steady press of man, his mechanical arm cutting through the thinnest slip of sand between cities. No more natural than this causeway, fit in steel and concrete, upon which we now pause. Great skeins of standing water plait and unplait themselves beneath us, negotiating this twin-mouthed threshold, open to the ocean and the bouy-studded bay. And still, the sun lights the water, the sluiced rocks, and from this glassy stretch of rain-damp road we can almost taste the night. Low in the waterlocked sky, the sun sounds like a first note in a dimmed theatre, wavering in tremolo before breaking into pieces.

AT SANKATY HEAD LIGHT

Under threat of rain, waiting for the sky
to break over this point, I tell myself a story.
Once they picked up the lighthouse whole,
broke it from its perch on the bluff
and delivered it inland while the whole sea watched,
worrying the shoreline with long fingers. Some afternoons
I found myself there, waiting for the sun
to break and thinking
of when I was small enough to fit in my brother's lap,
how he made me a sandwich for free when he worked
at Claudette's and I pulled a lemonade from the cooler,
popped open its metal cap on the footbridge south of town.
Or later, when he worked at the Chanticleer,
where in front an angry carousel horse brayed.
Strange how what I remember now is that animal's snarl
reaching towards the cobblestone rotary
where my brother would not hold my hand
as we walked down the middle of the road.
Is it that memory lives in the flesh, in the tongue
as taste fighting towards expression,
not words so much as a shadow of rosehips
squalling along the bluff, the particular weight
of bayberries wrapped in my mother's handkerchief,
the lichenous crack of a dry limb under my tennis shoe?
In the kitchen my brother unthreaded veins from shrimp
and the vermillion sky swore over the rooftops.
How much can we truly remember? Floorboards,
a sunlit shell, sand pine at the property's edge,

how the lighthouse broke the sky in two.
But then, all experience
is a story our remembered selves grow weary of telling,
dredging the ocean floor for recollections
compressed under the water's weight.
I think of my brother in stripes of light,
in shadows reaching across the lawn towards the lighthouse.
Once at midday a cop delivered him to our cottage,
my mother so severe. He had broken
into an abandoned home up the bluff, ocean wailing at his back.
Why did he do it? What does he remember, I wonder—
his red polo, brilliant in the sun, his inadvertent regret,
how I watched him straighten?
Barefoot, I ran in circles around them—
my mother, the cop, my brother, dark as crows
in the billowing grass—my arms out
like a plane waiting to be shot down.
At least, that's the story
I tell myself, delivered over and over
from the dark edge of the bluff
while the sea attends to its longings.

POINT OF SAIL (II)

I, too, am revolving.
I return here when I crave an answer,
converging and digressing in murmurs,
filling this space with lungs, sails, suns—like thoughts
revolving in invisible columns of air.
On the opposite shore
we sit in the muck of a sun-burned basin
carried in the arms of mangrove.
The light plucks those delicious leaves,
glancing off the water, and we dig in
as the sun empties itself into the bay.
The sky deepens like a well,
and now the first few southern stars, reminding me
of a video I watched—man freediving
into a blue hole west of Clarence Town
sunk 200 meters into the ocean floor.
He fell through the dark water until nothing was left
but four dim points of light
reflected from his hands and soles.
His weightlessness frightened me.
Watching the sky light up, I could tell you all this,
but the words seem
as clumsy as wanting
to place a finger on a single star
in the haze of the Milky Way,
and from our backs we can see that same swath of stars
pouring the sky into our tent.
I won't step into the water now,

the city a neon sigh,
thumbprint below this dark map,
charted by a wanting deeper than logic.
Instead, I ask you question after question:
the water, the sand, the caustic shimmer in the distance.
These questions are never the point.
They barrel through understanding
like an unmoored boat
drifting through someone else's dreams.
On the other side of the gravel path
that circles our tent, our own boat pulls
against its dock lines,
turning in some unknown wind,
buoyed by the salt-filled water
like a word on my next breath
that rolls, uncertain, but content
in its pitch, its revolutions,
while we balance in the vast wake of sky.

CPSIA information can be obtained
at www.ICGtesting.com
Printed in the USA
LVOW11s0505260917
550070LV00001B/41/P